SHARK
MOVES OUT
of the OCEAN

T0084477

by Nikki Potts • illustrated by Maarten Lenoir

PICTURE WINDOW BOOKS
a capstone imprint

Left fin, right fin.

Left fin, right fin.

Ocean ahead. Ocean behind.
Ocean everywhere!

Shark loves her warm,
watery home.

But the ocean
    is a quiet place.

Shark wants some
    excitement!

Shark's first stop is
the Amazon River.

Maybe she can find
adventure here!

Check out these fish!
They look like they
swim on the wild side.

Maybe they are
a little TOO wild
for Shark.

This ride looks like a thrill!
Shark hops in.

Next stop,
Niagara Falls!

The rapids are fast.
The drops are
exciting.

Getting splashed is cool.

This is the rush
Shark was missing
in the ocean!

Wait.
WAIT!

Shark wants off the ride!

EEEEEEEEEKKKKK!

Niagara Falls was
a little more adventure
than Shark was looking for.

Maybe a water park
will be a better fit.

Now this is
what Shark was
talking about!

SPLASH!

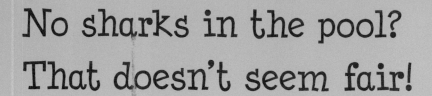

No sharks in the pool?
That doesn't seem fair!

Rules are rules though.
Shark needs to find a
new place to swim.

NO
SHARKS

22

Shark wants to give lake life a try. The neighbors look like they could use some help building their dam.

Shark is happy to lend a fin!

TA-DA!

Shark's talents are
not appreciated here.

Shark has had
enough excitement.

She is ready to
return home.

Until the next
great adventure . . .

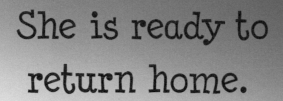

ALL ABOUT SHARKS

Great white sharks are the largest predatory fish on Earth.

Because they are so big, great white sharks have few natural enemies.

Great white sharks have about 300 teeth.

Sharks, including great whites, have been around for millions of years.

Scientists don't know much about great white sharks. Since they are at the top of the food chain, their population is small.

ANIMAL PASSPORT

Name: Great White Shark

Type: fish

Habitat: ocean

Diet: fish, stingrays, seals, sea lions, other sharks

Length: 21 feet (6.4 meters)

Weight: between 1,500 and 5,000 pounds (680 and 2,268 kilograms)

Lifespan: 70 years

Favorite activity: swimming

BOOKS IN THIS SERIES

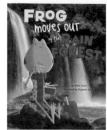  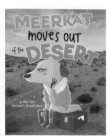  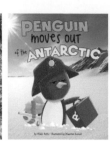 

Habitat Hunter is published by Picture Window Books, an imprint of Capstone.
1710 Roe Crest Drive
North Mankato, Minnesota 56003
www.capstonepub.com

**Library of Congress Cataloging-in-Publication Data is available
on the Library of Congress website.**
ISBN: 978-1-9771-1420-4 (library binding)
ISBN: 978-1-9771-2018-2 (paperback)
ISBN: 978-1-9771-1426-6 (eBook PDF)

Summary: Shark is bored with its habitat! Follow Shark as it tries out different places to live. Which habitat will make the best home for Shark?

Image Credits
Shutterstock: Andrey Armyagov, 10-11, Andrey Novgorodtsev, 8-9, Chase Dekker, 27, Don Tran, 18-19, Enrique Aguirre, 24-25, Jacomo, 20-21, jonnyslav, 22-23, littlesam, cover, Itummy, 6-7, Marek Poplawski, 12-13, Mauricio Graiki, 28-29, otorongo, 6-7, Paul Looyen, 16-17, Pi-Lenws, 26, Rich Carey, 2-3, Tatiana Popova, 4-5, Vector8DIY, back cover, vvital, 14-15, wavebreakmedia, 23, wildestanimal, 31

Artistic elements: pingebat, Valeriya_Dor

Editorial Credits
Editor: Mari Bolte; Designer: Kayla Rossow; Media Researcher: Kelly Garvin;
Production Specialist: Tori Abraham

All internet sites appearing in back matter were available
and accurate when this book was sent to press.